Breaking Through Executive Dysfunction

Strategiues For Patients with Complex Trauma and ADHD

Andrew D Beattie

First Edition 2023

Success Publications SAR

ISBN: 9782321209560

Table Of Contents

Strategies for managing executive dysfunction 44

Strategies for developing self-care practices that work for you

64

Introduction

Overview of the book

"Breaking Through Executive Dysfunction: Strategies for Patients with Complex Trauma and ADHD" is a book that offers a comprehensive overview of the challenges faced by individuals dealing with complex trauma and undiagnosed ADHD. The book provides practical strategies and coping mechanisms to help patients navigate through their daily lives.

The impact of complex trauma on ADHD symptoms and vice versa is a key focus of this book. The authors delve into the complexities of how these two conditions interact and the ways in which they can exacerbate each other. The book highlights the importance of seeking therapy to manage these conditions and offers guidance on how to find the right therapist.

Strategies for managing executive dysfunction in individuals with complex trauma and ADHD are also a key focus of this book. The authors provide practical tips for managing time, prioritizing tasks, and staying organized. They also offer advice on how to build healthy habits and routines that can help individuals with these conditions stay on track.

The link between complex trauma, ADHD, and anxiety is another important topic that the book covers. The authors explore how these conditions are interconnected and offer strategies for managing anxiety symptoms. They also provide tips for building resilience and coping with stress.

The impact of complex trauma and ADHD on relationships and social interactions is a key concern for many patients. The book offers guidance on how to build healthy relationships and improve social skills. It provides practical tips for communicating effectively and building trust.

The importance of self-care practices for individuals with complex trauma and ADHD is also emphasized in this book. The authors provide guidance on how to take care of oneself physically, emotionally, and mentally. They offer tips for building self-esteem and improving self-confidence.

The role of medication in managing ADHD symptoms in individuals with complex trauma is also discussed in this book. The authors provide guidance on how to find the right medication and the importance of working closely with a healthcare provider.

Finally, the impact of childhood trauma on ADHD diagnosis and treatment is an important topic that the book covers. The authors provide guidance on how to identify childhood trauma and its impact on ADHD symptoms. They also offer strategies for managing the long-term effects of childhood trauma.

Overall, "Breaking Through Executive Dysfunction: Strategies for Patients with Complex Trauma and ADHD" is a comprehensive guide that offers practical strategies and coping mechanisms for individuals dealing with these conditions. It is an essential resource for anyone seeking to improve their quality of life and build resilience in the face of adversity.

Explanation of complex trauma and ADHD

Explanation of Complex Trauma and ADHD

Complex trauma and attention-deficit/hyperactivity disorder (ADHD) are two conditions that often occur together. Complex trauma refers to prolonged exposure to traumatic events, such as physical, sexual, or emotional abuse. ADHD, on the other hand, is a neurodevelopmental disorder characterized by inattention, hyperactivity, and impulsivity.

The impact of complex trauma on ADHD symptoms can be significant. For example, individuals with complex trauma may have difficulty with attention and concentration due to their exposure to stressful and traumatic events. They may also have difficulty regulating their emotions and behaviors, leading to impulsivity and hyperactivity.

Similarly, ADHD can exacerbate the symptoms of complex trauma. Impulsivity and hyperactivity can lead to risky behaviors and poor decision-making, which can increase exposure to traumatic events. Inattention can also make it difficult to process and cope with traumatic experiences.

Therapy can be an effective tool for managing both complex trauma and ADHD. Cognitive-behavioral therapy (CBT) and trauma-focused therapy can help individuals process traumatic experiences and develop coping strategies. ADHD coaching and behavioral therapy can also help individuals with ADHD learn skills to manage their symptoms.

Self-care practices are also essential for individuals with complex trauma and ADHD. Regular exercise, healthy eating, and stress-reduction techniques such as mindfulness and meditation can help regulate emotions and improve overall well-being.

Medication can also be helpful for managing ADHD symptoms, but it is important to work closely with a healthcare provider to ensure proper dosing and to monitor for potential side effects.

Childhood trauma can also impact ADHD diagnosis and treatment. It is important for healthcare providers to screen for trauma history when evaluating individuals for ADHD, as trauma can mimic ADHD symptoms.

In conclusion, complex trauma and ADHD often occur together and can have a significant impact on an individual's well-being. Therapy, self-care practices, and medication can all be helpful tools for managing symptoms and improving overall functioning. It is important to work closely with healthcare providers to develop a comprehensive treatment plan that addresses both conditions.

Dealing with Complex Trauma and Undiagnosed ADHD

Understanding complex trauma and ADHD

Understanding Complex Trauma and ADHD

Individuals who have experienced complex trauma often struggle with executive dysfunction and attention deficit hyperactivity disorder (ADHD) symptoms. These symptoms can make it difficult to complete tasks, concentrate, and manage daily life. Understanding the link between complex trauma and ADHD can help individuals cope with their symptoms and develop strategies to manage executive dysfunction.

Complex trauma refers to prolonged exposure to traumatic events, such as physical or emotional abuse, neglect, or violence. These experiences can have a lasting impact on an individual's mental health and well-being, leading to symptoms such as anxiety, depression, and PTSD. Additionally, people who have experienced complex trauma may also struggle with executive dysfunction and ADHD.

Executive dysfunction is a term used to describe difficulties with cognitive processes, such as planning, organizing, and problem-solving. People with ADHD may also exhibit executive dysfunction symptoms, such as forgetfulness, impulsivity, and distractibility. The overlap between complex trauma and ADHD symptoms can make it challenging for individuals to navigate their daily lives.

Therapy can be an effective tool for managing complex trauma and ADHD symptoms. A therapist can help individuals develop coping strategies to manage executive dysfunction, such as breaking tasks into smaller, more manageable steps. Additionally, therapy can help individuals address the emotional impact of trauma, reducing anxiety and depression symptoms.

Self-care practices, such as exercise, meditation, and mindfulness, can also be helpful for managing symptoms of complex trauma and ADHD. These practices can help reduce stress and improve focus. Additionally, medication can be an effective tool for managing ADHD symptoms in individuals with complex trauma.

It's essential to note that childhood trauma can impact ADHD diagnosis and treatment. Children who have experienced trauma may exhibit symptoms that mimic ADHD, such as hyperactivity and distractibility. It's essential to work with a mental health professional who understands the interplay between complex trauma and ADHD to ensure accurate diagnosis and treatment.

In conclusion, understanding the link between complex trauma and ADHD can help individuals develop strategies to manage executive dysfunction and improve their quality of life. Therapy, self-care practices, and medication can all be effective tools for managing symptoms. Working with a mental health professional who understands the impact of childhood trauma on ADHD diagnosis and treatment is crucial for accurate diagnosis and effective treatment. With the right tools and support, individuals with complex trauma and ADHD can break through executive dysfunction and achieve their goals.

Common symptoms of complex trauma and undiagnosed ADHD

Common symptoms of complex trauma and undiagnosed ADHD

Complex trauma and undiagnosed ADHD often present with similar symptoms, making it difficult to differentiate between the two. While they are distinct conditions, they can overlap and exacerbate each other, creating a complex and challenging experience for patients. In this subchapter, we will explore some of the common symptoms of complex trauma and undiagnosed ADHD, and how they interact with each other.

One of the most common symptoms of complex trauma is hypervigilance. This is a state of constant alertness, where the patient feels like they are always on edge and ready for danger. It can be exhausting and overwhelming, and often leads to anxiety and panic attacks. Patients with undiagnosed ADHD may also experience hypervigilance, but for different reasons. ADHD patients often struggle with sensory overload and have difficulty filtering out irrelevant stimuli, which can lead to a feeling of being constantly overwhelmed and on edge.

Another common symptom of both complex trauma and ADHD is difficulty with attention and focus. Patients with complex trauma may struggle to concentrate due to intrusive thoughts and memories, while ADHD patients may have difficulty sustaining attention on tasks they find boring or uninteresting. This can lead to procrastination, poor academic or work performance, and frustration for both the patient and those around them.

Impulsivity is another hallmark symptom of ADHD, but it can also be present in patients with complex trauma. Trauma survivors may act impulsively as a coping mechanism, engaging in risky or self-destructive behaviors as a way to numb or escape their pain. ADHD patients may act impulsively due to poor impulse control and difficulty with delayed gratification.

Finally, both complex trauma and ADHD can impact social interactions and relationships. Trauma survivors may struggle with trust and intimacy, while ADHD patients may struggle to read social cues and maintain focus during conversations. This can lead to isolation and feelings of loneliness, which can exacerbate symptoms of both conditions.

It's important to note that while these symptoms are common in both complex trauma and ADHD, they are not necessarily indicative of either condition. If you are experiencing any of these symptoms, it's important to seek professional help to determine the root cause of your struggles and develop an individualized treatment plan.

Strategies for coping with complex trauma and undiagnosed ADHD

Strategies for Coping with Complex Trauma and Undiagnosed ADHD

Living with complex trauma and undiagnosed ADHD can be challenging. The symptoms of these conditions can often overlap, making it difficult to identify and manage them. However, there are several strategies that individuals can use to cope with these conditions and improve their overall quality of life.

1. Seek therapy: Therapy can be a valuable tool for individuals with complex trauma and undiagnosed ADHD. A trained therapist can help you identify and manage your symptoms, as well as work through any underlying issues that may be contributing to your condition.

2. Practice self-care: Self-care practices can help you manage the symptoms of complex trauma and ADHD. This may include activities like exercise, meditation, or journaling. It's important to find activities that you enjoy and that help you feel calm and centered.

3. Develop a routine: A routine can help individuals with complex trauma and ADHD manage executive dysfunction. By creating a schedule for your day, you can minimize distractions and stay focused on your tasks.

4. Use reminders: Reminders can be a helpful tool for individuals with ADHD. This may include setting alarms or using sticky notes to remind you of important tasks or appointments.

5. Communicate with loved ones: Complex trauma and ADHD can have a significant impact on relationships and social interactions. It's important to communicate with your loved ones about your condition and how it affects you. This can help them better understand your needs and provide support when you need it.

6. Consider medication: Medication can be an effective tool for managing ADHD symptoms in individuals with complex trauma. However, it's important to work closely with a healthcare provider to find the right medication and dosage for your needs.

7. Practice mindfulness: Mindfulness can help individuals with complex trauma and ADHD stay focused and present in the moment. This may include activities like deep breathing or guided meditation.

In conclusion, living with complex trauma and undiagnosed ADHD can be challenging, but there are several strategies that individuals can use to cope with these conditions and improve their overall quality of life. By seeking therapy, practicing self-care, developing a routine, using reminders, communicating with loved ones, considering medication, and practicing mindfulness, individuals can manage their symptoms and live a fulfilling life.

Coping Strategies for Individuals with Complex Trauma and Undiagnosed ADHD

Developing coping strategies for daily life

Developing coping strategies for daily life is an essential part of managing the symptoms of complex trauma and undiagnosed ADHD. Coping strategies refer to the techniques that individuals can use to deal with the challenges and stressors they encounter in their daily lives.

One of the most effective coping strategies for individuals with complex trauma and ADHD is to identify their triggers. Triggers refer to the situations, people, or events that lead to a negative emotional response, such as anxiety, anger, or sadness. Once an individual has identified their triggers, they can learn to avoid them or develop strategies to manage their emotional response.

Another strategy is to practice mindfulness. Mindfulness involves paying attention to the present moment without judgment. This technique can help individuals with complex trauma and ADHD to reduce their stress levels and improve their ability to focus.

Exercise is also an effective coping strategy for individuals with complex trauma and ADHD. Exercise releases endorphins, which are natural chemicals that improve mood and reduce stress. Regular exercise can also improve sleep and reduce symptoms of anxiety and depression.

Developing a support network is another essential coping strategy. This network can include family members, friends, therapists, or support groups. Having people who understand the challenges of complex trauma and ADHD can provide emotional support and practical help when needed.

Finally, individuals with complex trauma and ADHD can benefit from developing a self-care routine. Self-care refers to the activities that individuals engage in to promote their physical and emotional well-being. Examples of self-care activities include journaling, meditation, taking a relaxing bath, or engaging in a hobby.

In conclusion, developing coping strategies for daily life is crucial for individuals with complex trauma and undiagnosed ADHD. By identifying triggers, practicing mindfulness, exercising, developing a support network, and engaging in self-care activities, individuals can improve their ability to manage their symptoms and lead fulfilling lives. It is essential to remember that coping strategies are not a one-size-fits-all solution, and it may take time and experimentation to find what works best for each individual.

Practical tips for managing executive dysfunction

Practical Tips for Managing Executive Dysfunction

Executive dysfunction is a common symptom of complex trauma and ADHD. It can make it difficult to organize, plan, prioritize, and complete tasks. However, there are practical tips that can help individuals manage this symptom and improve their daily functioning. Here are some recommendations:

1. Use visual aids: Visual aids such as calendars, to-do lists, and reminders can be helpful in keeping track of tasks and deadlines. They can also serve as a visual reminder of progress and accomplishments.

2. Break tasks into smaller steps: Large tasks can be overwhelming and lead to procrastination. Breaking them into smaller steps can make them more manageable and less intimidating.

3. Set realistic goals: It is important to set goals that are achievable and realistic. This can help reduce the likelihood of feeling overwhelmed and increase motivation.

4. Use positive self-talk: Negative self-talk can be a barrier to progress and success. Using positive self-talk can help increase self-esteem and motivation.

5. Practice self-care: Self-care practices such as exercise, meditation, and healthy eating can improve overall health and well-being. This can lead to increased energy and motivation to complete tasks.

6. Seek therapy: Therapy can be a valuable tool in managing executive dysfunction. A therapist can provide strategies and support to improve daily functioning and address underlying issues related to trauma and ADHD.

7. Consider medication: Medication can be helpful in managing ADHD symptoms. It is important to work with a healthcare professional to determine the appropriate medication and dosage.

8. Communicate with others: Communication with others can help reduce isolation and increase support. It is important to communicate needs and limitations with family, friends, and coworkers.

9. Practice mindfulness: Mindfulness can be helpful in reducing stress and increasing focus. It involves being present in the moment and non-judgmentally observing thoughts and feelings.

10. Celebrate accomplishments: Celebrating accomplishments, no matter how small, can increase motivation and self-esteem. It is important to recognize progress and successes.

Managing executive dysfunction can be challenging, but with the right strategies and support, it is possible to improve daily functioning and overall well-being. It is important to remember that progress takes time and patience, and to seek help when needed.

Strategies for improving focus and concentration

Strategies for improving focus and concentration are essential for individuals dealing with complex trauma and undiagnosed ADHD. Executive dysfunction can make it challenging to concentrate on tasks and stay focused for extended periods. However, with the right strategies, it is possible to improve focus and concentration. Here are some tips to help you:

1. Get organized - One of the most effective ways to improve focus and concentration is by getting organized. This means creating a schedule and sticking to it, decluttering your workspace, and breaking down tasks into smaller, more manageable chunks.

2. Use visual aids - Visual aids can help individuals with complex trauma and ADHD stay focused and on task. These aids could include a whiteboard, sticky notes, or a planner.

3. Remove distractions - Distractions can be detrimental to focus and concentration. Therefore, it is crucial to remove them as much as possible. This includes turning off your phone, closing unnecessary tabs on your computer, and finding a quiet workspace.

4. Take breaks - Taking regular breaks can help you recharge and stay focused. It is recommended that you take a break every 45-60 minutes to rest and recharge.

5. Use mindfulness techniques - Mindfulness techniques can help you stay present and focused. These techniques could include deep breathing, meditation, or yoga.

6. Exercise - Exercise is a great way to boost focus and concentration. Regular exercise can help reduce stress and improve cognitive function.

7. Get enough sleep - Sleep is crucial for cognitive function. Individuals with complex trauma and ADHD should aim to get at least seven hours of sleep each night.

In conclusion, improving focus and concentration is crucial for individuals with complex trauma and undiagnosed ADHD. By getting organized, using visual aids, removing distractions, taking breaks, using mindfulness techniques, exercising, and getting enough sleep, it is possible to improve focus and concentration. These strategies can help individuals with complex trauma and ADHD manage their symptoms and improve their overall quality of life.

The Impact of Complex Trauma on ADHD Symptoms and Vice Versa

Exploring the relationship between complex trauma and ADHD

Exploring the relationship between complex trauma and ADHD

The relationship between complex trauma and ADHD is complex and multifaceted. While both conditions are distinct, they often occur together, with one exacerbating the other. Individuals with complex trauma experience a range of symptoms, including anxiety, depression, and dissociation, which can lead to difficulty with attention, memory, and executive function. Similarly, ADHD can cause impairments in attention, impulse control, and hyperactivity, which can exacerbate the symptoms of complex trauma.

One of the key challenges in managing complex trauma and ADHD is recognizing the interplay between the two conditions. For individuals who are dealing with complex trauma and undiagnosed ADHD, it can be difficult to distinguish between symptoms of trauma and symptoms of ADHD. This can lead to misdiagnosis or underdiagnosis, which can hinder effective treatment.

Coping strategies for individuals with complex trauma and undiagnosed ADHD should include a multifaceted approach that addresses both conditions. Therapy is a critical component of this approach, as it can help individuals process their trauma and develop coping strategies for managing ADHD symptoms. Additionally, strategies for managing executive dysfunction, such as creating a structured routine, setting achievable goals, and using visual aids, can be helpful for individuals with both conditions.

The link between complex trauma, ADHD, and anxiety is well-established. Individuals with complex trauma are at a higher risk for developing anxiety disorders, which can further exacerbate the symptoms of ADHD. Similarly, individuals with ADHD are at a higher risk for developing anxiety disorders, which can further impair their ability to manage the symptoms of complex trauma.

The impact of complex trauma and ADHD on relationships and social interactions is also significant. Individuals with complex trauma may struggle with trust, intimacy, and emotional regulation, which can make it difficult to form and maintain healthy relationships. Similarly, individuals with ADHD may struggle with impulse control, social skills, and emotional regulation, which can also hinder their ability to form and maintain healthy relationships.

Self-care practices are critical for individuals with complex trauma and ADHD. These practices can include mindfulness, exercise, healthy eating, and relaxation techniques. Additionally, medication can be an effective tool for managing ADHD symptoms in individuals with complex trauma, although it should be used in conjunction with therapy and lifestyle changes.

Finally, it is important to recognize the impact of childhood trauma on ADHD diagnosis and treatment. Children who experience trauma are at a higher risk for developing ADHD, and may require different treatment approaches than children who do not have a history of trauma.

In conclusion, exploring the relationship between complex trauma and ADHD is crucial for effective diagnosis and treatment. By recognizing the interplay between these two conditions, individuals can develop a multifaceted approach that addresses both the symptoms of trauma and ADHD. This approach should include therapy, coping strategies, self-care practices, medication, and lifestyle changes. With the right tools and support, individuals with complex trauma and ADHD can successfully manage their symptoms and live fulfilling lives.

Understanding how complex trauma can impact ADHD symptoms

Understanding how complex trauma can impact ADHD symptoms

Complex trauma, also called developmental trauma, refers to prolonged exposure to traumatic experiences during childhood, such as neglect, abuse, or abandonment. These experiences can shape the way our brain develops, leading to long-lasting effects on our mental health and behavior. One of the ways complex trauma can manifest itself is through symptoms of attention-deficit/hyperactivity disorder (ADHD).

ADHD is a neurodevelopmental disorder that affects attention, impulse control, and hyperactivity. It can be challenging to diagnose, especially in individuals who have experienced complex trauma. The symptoms of ADHD, such as difficulty focusing, forgetfulness, and impulsivity, can also be present in those who have experienced trauma. As a result, it is essential to understand how complex trauma can impact ADHD symptoms to receive an accurate diagnosis and effective treatment.

Research shows that children who have experienced trauma are more likely to develop symptoms of ADHD than those who have not. The impact of trauma on the brain can lead to difficulties with executive functioning, which is the ability to plan, organize, and prioritize tasks. These difficulties can mimic the symptoms of ADHD, leading to a misdiagnosis.

Moreover, the symptoms of ADHD can exacerbate the effects of trauma. For example, individuals with ADHD may struggle in school or work, leading to feelings of frustration and low self-esteem. These feelings can compound the effects of trauma, making it harder for individuals to cope with their experiences.

Therapy is an essential tool for managing the impact of complex trauma and ADHD on an individual's life. A therapist can help individuals develop coping strategies for managing their symptoms, improve their executive functioning skills, and address the underlying trauma that may be contributing to their symptoms.

Additionally, self-care practices such as exercise, meditation, and healthy eating can help individuals manage the effects of trauma and ADHD. These practices can improve mood, reduce stress, and increase overall well-being.

In some cases, medication may be necessary to manage the symptoms of ADHD in individuals with complex trauma. However, medication should be used in conjunction with therapy and other self-care practices for the most effective treatment.

Ultimately, understanding the link between complex trauma and ADHD is crucial for individuals seeking to manage their symptoms. By addressing the underlying trauma and developing effective coping strategies, individuals can improve their overall well-being and lead fulfilling lives.

Strategies for managing symptoms of both complex trauma and ADHD

Strategies for managing symptoms of both complex trauma and ADHD

Dealing with complex trauma and undiagnosed ADHD can be challenging for patients. The symptoms of both conditions can cause difficulties with executive functioning, attention, and emotional regulation. However, there are effective strategies that individuals can use to manage these symptoms and improve their quality of life.

Coping strategies for individuals with complex trauma and undiagnosed ADHD

One of the most effective coping strategies for individuals with complex trauma and ADHD is to develop a daily routine. This routine can include prioritizing tasks, creating a schedule, and setting reminders for important events. By establishing a routine, individuals can reduce stress and anxiety and increase their ability to focus and complete tasks.

Another strategy is to practice mindfulness meditation. Mindfulness can help individuals regulate their emotions, decrease impulsivity, and improve attention. Mindfulness can be practiced through guided meditation, yoga, or simply taking a few minutes each day to breathe and focus on the present moment.

The impact of complex trauma on ADHD symptoms and vice versa

Complex trauma can have a significant impact on ADHD symptoms. Trauma can lead to hyperarousal, hypervigilance, and emotional dysregulation, all of which can exacerbate ADHD symptoms. Conversely, ADHD symptoms can make it more difficult for individuals to cope with trauma by impairing their ability to focus, regulate emotions, and form stable relationships.

The role of therapy in managing complex trauma and undiagnosed ADHD

Therapy can be an effective tool for managing both complex trauma and ADHD. Cognitive-behavioral therapy (CBT) can help individuals develop coping skills and improve their executive functioning. Eye Movement Desensitization and Reprocessing (EMDR) can help individuals process traumatic memories and reduce the impact of trauma on their daily lives.

Strategies for managing executive dysfunction in individuals with complex trauma and ADHD

Executive dysfunction is a common symptom of both complex trauma and ADHD. To manage executive dysfunction, individuals can use tools such as calendars, task lists, and alarms to help them stay organized and focused. They may also benefit from cognitive rehabilitation therapy, which can help them develop specific skills related to attention, memory, and organization.

The link between complex trauma, ADHD, and anxiety

There is a strong link between complex trauma, ADHD, and anxiety. Trauma can increase anxiety symptoms, which can exacerbate ADHD symptoms. Anxiety can also make it more difficult for individuals to regulate their emotions and focus on tasks.

The impact of complex trauma and ADHD on relationships and social interactions

Both complex trauma and ADHD can have a significant impact on relationships and social interactions. Individuals with these conditions may struggle to form and maintain relationships due to difficulties with emotional regulation, communication, and social cues.

The importance of self-care practices for individuals with complex trauma and ADHD

Self-care practices are essential for individuals with complex trauma and ADHD. These practices can include exercise, healthy eating, mindfulness, and relaxation techniques. Self-care practices can help individuals reduce stress and anxiety, improve their mood, and increase their ability to focus and complete tasks.

The role of medication in managing ADHD symptoms in individuals with complex trauma

Medication can be an effective tool for managing ADHD symptoms in individuals with complex trauma. However, medication should be used in conjunction with therapy and other coping strategies to achieve the best results.

The impact of childhood trauma on ADHD diagnosis and treatment

Childhood trauma can have a significant impact on the diagnosis and treatment of ADHD. Trauma can lead to difficulties with attention, emotional regulation, and executive functioning, which can be mistaken for ADHD symptoms. It is important for clinicians to consider a patient's history of trauma when diagnosing and treating ADHD.

In conclusion, managing complex trauma and ADHD can be challenging, but there are effective strategies that individuals can use to improve their quality of life. By developing a routine, practicing mindfulness, using therapy and medication, and engaging in self-care practices, individuals can reduce symptoms, improve their executive functioning, and build healthy relationships.

The Role of Therapy in Managing Complex Trauma and Undiagnosed ADHD

Overview of therapy options

Overview of Therapy Options

For individuals dealing with complex trauma and undiagnosed ADHD, therapy can be a vital tool in managing symptoms and improving overall well-being. There are several different types of therapy options available, each with its own unique benefits and drawbacks.

Cognitive Behavioral Therapy (CBT) is a common form of therapy that is often used to treat both complex trauma and ADHD. CBT focuses on identifying negative thought patterns and behaviors and replacing them with more positive ones. This can be particularly helpful for individuals who struggle with executive dysfunction, as it can help them develop strategies for managing their time and priorities more effectively.

Eye Movement Desensitization and Reprocessing (EMDR) is another therapy option that can be particularly effective for individuals with complex trauma. EMDR involves guided eye movements that are designed to help the brain reprocess traumatic memories in a more adaptive way. This can help reduce symptoms of anxiety, depression, and other emotional disturbances that can be associated with trauma.

Dialectical Behavior Therapy (DBT) is another type of therapy that can be helpful for individuals with complex trauma and ADHD. DBT focuses on developing skills in mindfulness, emotional regulation, interpersonal effectiveness, and distress tolerance. This can be particularly helpful for individuals who struggle with impulsivity or emotional dysregulation.

In addition to these therapy options, there are also a number of self-care practices that can be helpful for individuals with complex trauma and ADHD. These may include things like regular exercise, healthy eating, mindfulness meditation, and spending time in nature.

It is important to note that medication can also be an important tool in managing ADHD symptoms in individuals with complex trauma. However, medication should always be used in conjunction with therapy and other supportive interventions, as it is not a cure-all solution.

Overall, therapy can be an important tool in managing the complex symptoms that can be associated with trauma and ADHD. By working with a skilled therapist, individuals can develop strategies for managing executive dysfunction, reducing anxiety, improving relationships, and improving overall well-being.

How therapy can help with complex trauma and ADHD

Therapy can be a powerful tool for individuals who are dealing with complex trauma and undiagnosed ADHD. The impact of complex trauma on ADHD symptoms and vice versa can be significant, and therapy can help patients to better understand and manage these challenges.

One of the key roles of therapy in managing complex trauma and undiagnosed ADHD is to help patients develop coping strategies that can be used in daily life. This might include techniques for managing anxiety or stress, strategies for improving executive functioning, or tools for improving communication and social interaction skills.

Therapy can also be useful in helping patients to identify and manage the link between complex trauma, ADHD, and anxiety. Patients with complex trauma may be more prone to anxiety, and this can exacerbate ADHD symptoms. By working with a therapist, patients can learn to recognize these patterns and develop strategies for managing their symptoms.

In addition to these more practical benefits, therapy can also play an important role in helping patients to build stronger relationships and improve their social interactions. Individuals with complex trauma and ADHD may struggle with social cues or have difficulty connecting with others. Through therapy, patients can learn to better understand themselves and their relationships, and develop skills for communicating more effectively with others.

Self-care practices are also an essential aspect of managing complex trauma and ADHD, and therapy can help patients to develop a self-care routine that works for them. This might include mindfulness practices, exercise or other physical activities, or simply taking time for themselves to relax and recharge.

For some patients with complex trauma and ADHD, medication may also be an important part of their treatment plan. A therapist can work with patients to help them understand the benefits and risks of different medications, and to ensure that they are being used safely and effectively.

Finally, it's important to recognize the impact that childhood trauma can have on ADHD diagnosis and treatment. By working with a therapist who specializes in these areas, patients can gain a greater understanding of their own experiences and how they may be affecting their current challenges. With this knowledge, patients can take steps towards healing and begin to build a brighter future.

Finding the right therapist for you

Finding the right therapist for you is an essential step in managing complex trauma and ADHD. Therapy can help individuals with complex trauma and undiagnosed ADHD to develop coping strategies, manage executive dysfunction, and improve their overall mental health.

When searching for a therapist, it is important to consider their experience and expertise in treating complex trauma and ADHD. Look for a therapist who has specialized training or certification in these areas, as they will have a deeper understanding of the unique challenges that patients with these conditions face.

It is also important to consider the therapeutic approach of the therapist. Some therapists may use cognitive-behavioral therapy, while others may use psychodynamic therapy. Research different approaches and decide which one resonates with you the most.

Another important factor to consider is the personality and communication style of the therapist. A good therapist should make you feel comfortable, safe, and heard. They should be able to create a space where you feel free to express yourself without judgment.

It is also important to consider practical factors such as location, cost, and availability. You want to find a therapist who is convenient for you to see and who fits within your budget.

Don't be afraid to ask questions and interview potential therapists before making a decision. Ask about their experience, approach, and how they would approach your specific situation.

In addition to therapy, it is important to practice self-care strategies such as exercise, mindfulness, and relaxation techniques. These practices can help individuals with complex trauma and ADHD to manage symptoms and improve overall well-being.

While medication can be helpful in managing ADHD symptoms, it is important to work with a qualified healthcare professional to determine the best course of treatment. Childhood trauma can impact ADHD diagnosis and treatment, so it is important to be open and honest with healthcare professionals about your history.

In summary, finding the right therapist for you is a crucial step in managing complex trauma and ADHD. Consider factors such as experience, therapeutic approach, communication style, and practical considerations when selecting a therapist. In addition, practice self-care strategies and work with healthcare professionals to determine the best course of treatment.

Strategies for Managing Executive Dysfunction in Individuals with Complex Trauma and ADHD

Understanding executive dysfunction

Understanding Executive Dysfunction

Executive dysfunction is a common phenomenon experienced by individuals with complex trauma and ADHD. It is characterized by a set of cognitive impairments that affect a person's ability to initiate, plan, organize, and carry out tasks. Executive dysfunction can manifest itself in various ways, such as forgetfulness, procrastination, poor time management, lack of motivation, and difficulty in multitasking. In this subchapter, we will explore executive dysfunction and its impact on individuals with complex trauma and undiagnosed ADHD.

The Link between Complex Trauma, ADHD, and Executive Dysfunction

Executive dysfunction is closely linked to complex trauma and ADHD. Individuals who have experienced traumatic events in their lives may develop executive dysfunction as a coping mechanism. The brain's natural response to trauma is to shut down certain cognitive functions to protect the individual from further harm. As a result, executive functioning may become impaired, making it difficult for the person to manage their day-to-day tasks.

Similarly, individuals with ADHD have a pre-existing condition that affects their executive functioning. ADHD is a neurodevelopmental disorder that affects the brain's ability to regulate attention, impulse control, and hyperactivity. As a result, individuals with ADHD may find it challenging to focus on tasks, organize their thoughts, and manage their time effectively.

The Impact of Executive Dysfunction on Relationships and Social Interactions

Executive dysfunction can have a significant impact on relationships and social interactions. Individuals with executive dysfunction may struggle to keep appointments, forget important dates, and fail to follow through on commitments. This can lead to frustration and disappointment from their friends, family, and colleagues.

In addition, individuals with executive dysfunction may have difficulty with social cues and non-verbal communication. This can lead to misunderstandings and misinterpretations, making it challenging to form and maintain relationships.

Strategies for Managing Executive Dysfunction

Managing executive dysfunction requires a multi-faceted approach. Therapy can be an essential tool in managing executive dysfunction. The therapist can help the individual develop coping mechanisms to manage their symptoms and develop strategies to improve their executive functioning.

Self-care practices can also be helpful in managing executive dysfunction. Exercise, meditation, and mindfulness can help reduce stress and improve cognitive function. Additionally, individuals with executive dysfunction can benefit from using tools such as calendars, to-do lists, and reminders to help them stay organized and manage their time effectively.

Conclusion

Executive dysfunction is a common experience for individuals with complex trauma and ADHD. It can have a significant impact on their daily lives, relationships, and social interactions. Understanding executive dysfunction and its link to complex trauma and ADHD is essential in developing effective coping mechanisms. Therapy, self-care practices, and tools such as calendars and reminders can be helpful in managing executive dysfunction and improving overall quality of life.

Strategies for managing executive dysfunction

Strategies for Managing Executive Dysfunction

Executive dysfunction is a common symptom of complex trauma and ADHD. It can make it challenging to manage tasks, follow through with plans, and maintain focus. Fortunately, there are strategies that can help patients manage executive dysfunction and take control of their lives.

1. Create a Daily Routine

A daily routine can help patients with executive dysfunction stay organized and on track. This routine should include a set wake-up time, meal times, and designated times for work or other activities. Patients should also schedule in breaks throughout the day to avoid burnout.

2. Break Tasks into Smaller Steps

Complex tasks can be overwhelming for patients with executive dysfunction. Breaking tasks into smaller, more manageable steps can make them feel less daunting and more achievable. Patients can also use a planner or calendar to keep track of their progress.

3. Use Visual Aids

Visual aids such as calendars, task lists, and reminder notes can be helpful for patients with executive dysfunction. These aids can serve as a visual reminder of what needs to be done and when. Patients can use different colors to differentiate between tasks and prioritize them accordingly.

4. Practice Mindfulness

Mindfulness practices such as meditation and deep breathing can help patients with executive dysfunction stay calm and focused. These practices can also help patients manage anxiety and stress, which can exacerbate executive dysfunction symptoms.

5. Seek Professional Help

Therapy can be a valuable tool for patients with executive dysfunction. A therapist can help patients identify triggers for executive dysfunction and develop coping strategies to manage symptoms. They can also provide support and guidance as patients work through their challenges.

In conclusion, managing executive dysfunction can be challenging, but with the right strategies, patients can take control of their lives and achieve their goals. Patients should create a daily routine, break tasks into smaller steps, use visual aids, practice mindfulness, and seek professional help to manage executive dysfunction effectively. By implementing these strategies, patients can overcome executive dysfunction and thrive despite complex trauma and ADHD.

How to prioritize tasks and stay organized

Prioritizing tasks and staying organized can be challenging for individuals with complex trauma and undiagnosed ADHD. Executive dysfunction can cause disorganization, forgetfulness, and difficulty with planning and prioritizing tasks. However, there are strategies that can help manage these symptoms and improve productivity.

One effective way to prioritize tasks is to use a to-do list. Writing down tasks and breaking them into smaller, more manageable steps can help prevent overwhelm and increase motivation. It's important to prioritize the most important tasks first and to be realistic about what can be accomplished in a given day.

Another strategy is to use a planner or calendar. This can help keep track of appointments, deadlines, and other important events. It's important to review the planner regularly and make adjustments as needed.

Creating a routine can also help with organization. Setting specific times for tasks such as exercise, meal planning, and cleaning can help create structure and increase productivity. It's important to be flexible and allow for adjustments as needed.

Using technology can also be helpful. There are many apps and tools available for task management, such as Trello and Asana. These can help with task tracking, project management, and collaboration.

It's important to take breaks and practice self-care. Taking breaks can help prevent burnout and increase productivity. Self-care practices such as exercise, mindfulness, and time spent in nature can help reduce stress and improve overall well-being.

Therapy can also be helpful in managing executive dysfunction. A therapist can provide support and guidance in developing strategies for managing symptoms and improving productivity. Medication may also be helpful in managing ADHD symptoms in individuals with complex trauma.

It's important to remember that managing executive dysfunction takes time and practice. It's important to be patient and compassionate with oneself and to celebrate small successes along the way. With the right strategies and support, individuals with complex trauma and undiagnosed ADHD can improve their ability to prioritize tasks and stay organized.

The Link Between Complex Trauma, ADHD, and Anxiety

Understanding the relationship between complex trauma, ADHD, and anxiety

Understanding the relationship between complex trauma, ADHD, and anxiety is essential for individuals with complex trauma and undiagnosed ADHD. Complex trauma refers to exposure to multiple traumatic events, such as physical, emotional, and sexual abuse, neglect, and other adverse experiences during childhood. ADHD, on the other hand, is a neurodevelopmental disorder characterized by inattention, hyperactivity, and impulsivity. Anxiety is a common symptom of both complex trauma and ADHD, often co-occurring with these conditions.

The impact of complex trauma on ADHD symptoms and vice versa is significant. Individuals with complex trauma may experience difficulties in attention, concentration, and executive function, which are also hallmarks of ADHD. They may display hyperarousal, hypervigilance, and emotional dysregulation, which can lead to distractibility, impulsivity, and restlessness. The overlap in symptoms can make it challenging to distinguish between ADHD and complex trauma, leading to misdiagnosis and inappropriate treatment.

The link between complex trauma, ADHD, and anxiety is multifaceted. Research suggests that childhood trauma increases the risk of developing ADHD and anxiety disorders. Individuals with ADHD may also be more vulnerable to traumatic experiences due to their impulsivity and risk-taking behaviors. Anxiety, characterized by excessive worry and fear, can exacerbate ADHD symptoms and contribute to executive dysfunction, such as procrastination and avoidance.

The role of therapy in managing complex trauma and undiagnosed ADHD cannot be overstated. Evidence-based treatments, such as trauma-focused cognitive-behavioral therapy and ADHD coaching, can help individuals develop coping strategies and improve executive function. Therapy can also address underlying emotional and relational issues that may contribute to complex trauma and ADHD symptoms.

Strategies for managing executive dysfunction in individuals with complex trauma and ADHD include establishing routines, breaking tasks into smaller steps, and using external aids, such as calendars and reminders. Self-care practices, such as exercise, mindfulness, and social support, can also alleviate anxiety and promote well-being.

The impact of childhood trauma on ADHD diagnosis and treatment highlights the need for a comprehensive assessment that considers the individual's developmental history and current symptoms. Medication can be a helpful adjunct to therapy for managing ADHD symptoms, but it should be used cautiously and under the supervision of a qualified healthcare professional.

In conclusion, understanding the relationship between complex trauma, ADHD, and anxiety is crucial for individuals with these conditions. Therapy, self-care practices, and medication can help manage symptoms and improve quality of life. It is essential to seek professional help and advocate for appropriate diagnosis and treatment to break through executive dysfunction and achieve optimal functioning.

Strategies for managing anxiety

Strategies for managing anxiety

Anxiety is a common symptom experienced by individuals with complex trauma and undiagnosed ADHD. It can be overwhelming and interfere with daily functioning. However, there are several strategies that can help manage anxiety.

1. Deep breathing exercises: Practicing deep breathing exercises can help calm the mind and body. Take deep breaths, hold for a few seconds, and exhale slowly. Repeat this exercise for a few minutes until you feel more relaxed.

2. Mindfulness meditation: Mindfulness meditation involves focusing on the present moment without judgment. It can help reduce anxiety and increase self-awareness. Find a quiet place, sit comfortably, and focus on your breath. If your mind wanders, gently bring it back to your breath.

3. Exercise: Exercise is a great way to reduce anxiety. It releases endorphins, which can improve mood and reduce stress. Find an exercise that you enjoy and make it a part of your daily routine.

4. Cognitive-behavioral therapy (CBT): CBT is a type of therapy that helps individuals identify and change negative thought patterns. It can be helpful in managing anxiety and other symptoms of complex trauma and ADHD.

5. Medication: In some cases, medication may be necessary to manage anxiety. Talk to your healthcare provider about your options.

6. Self-care: Practicing self-care is important for managing anxiety. Make time for activities that you enjoy, such as reading, listening to music, or taking a relaxing bath. Engage in positive self-talk and be kind to yourself.

7. Social support: Having a support system can help reduce anxiety. Reach out to friends and family members for support, or consider joining a support group for individuals with complex trauma and ADHD.

Remember, managing anxiety is a process and may require a combination of strategies. It is important to be patient and persistent in your efforts to manage anxiety. With time and practice, you can learn to cope with anxiety and improve your overall well-being.

The Impact of Complex Trauma and ADHD on Relationships and Social Interactions

Understanding how complex trauma and ADHD can impact relationships

Understanding how Complex Trauma and ADHD can Impact Relationships

Living with complex trauma and ADHD can be challenging, especially when it comes to interpersonal relationships. Both conditions can affect your ability to interact with others positively, leading to conflicts, misunderstandings, and emotional distress. In this subchapter, we will explore the ways in which complex trauma and ADHD can impact relationships and provide practical strategies for managing them.

Impact of Complex Trauma on Relationships

Complex trauma can make it hard for individuals to form healthy relationships. Trauma survivors may struggle with trust issues, feel disconnected from others, and fear abandonment. They may also have difficulty expressing their emotions or needs, leading to misunderstandings and conflicts in relationships. Trauma can also make individuals more vulnerable to abusive relationships or toxic friendships.

ADHD and Relationships

ADHD can also impact relationships negatively. People with ADHD may struggle with impulsivity, distraction, and poor time management, making it hard to keep up with social obligations or maintain regular communication with friends and family. They may also struggle with emotional regulation, leading to outbursts or overreactions in social situations.

The Link Between Complex Trauma, ADHD, and Relationships

The link between complex trauma and ADHD can further complicate relationships. Trauma can affect the brain's development, leading to executive dysfunction, which can mimic ADHD symptoms. Furthermore, ADHD can make trauma symptoms worse, leading to increased anxiety, depression, and emotional dysregulation. These factors can make it challenging for individuals to form and maintain healthy relationships.

Strategies for Managing Relationships

Managing relationships with complex trauma and ADHD requires self-awareness, communication, and boundary setting. It is essential to identify triggers that may lead to emotional dysregulation and communicate these triggers to loved ones. Setting boundaries can also help avoid conflicts and emotional distress. Finally, seeking therapy can help individuals learn effective communication strategies, emotional regulation techniques, and coping skills.

In conclusion, managing relationships with complex trauma and ADHD requires self-awareness, communication, and boundary setting. It is crucial to understand the impact of these conditions on relationships and seek professional help when needed. Remember, relationships take effort and patience, but with the right strategies, they can be rewarding and fulfilling.

Strategies for improving communication

Strategies for improving communication:

Effective communication is key to maintaining healthy relationships, both personal and professional. However, for individuals with complex trauma and undiagnosed ADHD, communication can be a challenge. Here are some strategies that can help improve communication:

1. Active listening: Active listening is a technique that involves fully engaging in the conversation and remaining focused on what the other person is saying. This means paying attention to both verbal and nonverbal cues, such as body language and tone of voice.

2. Clear communication: Individuals with complex trauma and ADHD may struggle with expressing themselves clearly. It is important to be concise, use simple language, and avoid jargon or complex vocabulary. Additionally, it is helpful to use visual aids, such as diagrams or illustrations, to help clarify your message.

3. Practice empathy: Empathy is the ability to understand and share the feelings of another person. It is important to practice empathy when communicating with others, especially if they are expressing strong emotions. This involves acknowledging their feelings and validating their experiences.

4. Ask questions: Asking questions is an effective way to ensure that you have understood the other person's message. It also shows that you are interested and engaged in the conversation. Be sure to ask open-ended questions, which encourage the other person to elaborate and provide more information.

5. Take breaks: Individuals with complex trauma and ADHD may become overwhelmed or overstimulated during a conversation. It is important to take breaks when needed, to process information and decompress.

Improving communication can be a challenging process, but with practice and patience, it is possible to develop effective communication skills. Remember to be patient with yourself and others, and to seek support from a therapist or counselor if needed.

Navigating social situations with complex trauma and ADHD

Navigating social situations with complex trauma and ADHD can be challenging for individuals who struggle with executive dysfunction. Social interactions can be overwhelming and trigger anxiety, leading to avoidance behaviors and isolation. However, with the right strategies and support, individuals with complex trauma and ADHD can learn to navigate social situations successfully.

One of the first steps in managing social situations is to identify triggers and plan ahead. For example, if large crowds are overwhelming, it may be helpful to avoid crowded places or attend events during off-peak hours. If socializing with new people is difficult, it may be helpful to practice introductions and small talk with a trusted friend or family member before attending an event.

Another useful strategy is to establish boundaries and communicate them clearly. Individuals with complex trauma and ADHD may struggle to say no or assert their needs, which can lead to overcommitment and burnout. It's important to prioritize self-care and set realistic expectations for social interactions.

Therapy can also play a crucial role in managing complex trauma and ADHD symptoms. A therapist can help individuals identify triggers, develop coping strategies, and improve communication skills. Through therapy, individuals can learn to regulate their emotions, improve self-esteem, and build healthier relationships.

In addition, medication can be an effective tool in managing ADHD symptoms, but it's important to work closely with a healthcare provider to find the right medication and dosage. Medication can help improve focus, reduce impulsivity, and increase motivation, which can help individuals feel more comfortable in social situations.

Finally, self-care practices are essential for individuals with complex trauma and ADHD. Regular exercise, healthy eating, and adequate sleep can help improve overall well-being and reduce stress. Engaging in hobbies and activities that bring joy and relaxation can also help improve mood and reduce anxiety.

In conclusion, navigating social situations with complex trauma and ADHD can be challenging, but with the right strategies and support, individuals can learn to overcome their difficulties and build healthy relationships. By identifying triggers, establishing boundaries, seeking therapy and medication when necessary, and prioritizing self-care, individuals can improve their executive function and lead fulfilling lives.

The Importance of Self-Care Practices for Individuals with Complex Trauma and ADHD

Overview of self-care practices

Overview of self-care practices

Self-care practices are an essential part of managing complex trauma and ADHD. They involve taking care of yourself physically, emotionally, and mentally to maintain your overall well-being. While it may seem challenging to prioritize self-care, it is crucial to make it a part of your daily routine, especially when dealing with complex trauma and undiagnosed ADHD.

Self-care practices can help you manage your symptoms and improve your quality of life. Here are some self-care practices that can help you cope with complex trauma and undiagnosed ADHD:

1. Exercise: Regular exercise can help manage ADHD symptoms by reducing hyperactivity and impulsivity. It can also help relieve anxiety and depression associated with complex trauma. Exercise also improves overall physical health, which can help boost mood and energy levels.

2. Sleep: Getting enough sleep is crucial for individuals with complex trauma and ADHD. Lack of sleep can worsen symptoms, such as inattention and impulsivity. It is essential to create a sleep routine and stick to it to ensure you get enough rest.

3. Mindfulness: Mindfulness practices, such as meditation, can help manage anxiety and stress. It can also help improve attention and focus.

4. Healthy diet: Eating a healthy diet can help improve overall well-being. Avoiding sugary foods and processed foods can help manage ADHD symptoms, while a balanced diet can help boost energy levels and improve mood.

5. Time management: Individuals with complex trauma and ADHD often struggle with time management. Creating a schedule and prioritizing tasks can help manage symptoms and improve productivity.

6. Social support: Having a support system can help manage the impact of complex trauma and ADHD on relationships and social interactions. It is essential to connect with others and build healthy relationships.

In conclusion, self-care practices are essential for managing complex trauma and ADHD. Incorporating these practices into your daily routine can help manage symptoms and improve overall well-being. It is crucial to prioritize self-care and make it a part of your daily routine to manage the impact of complex trauma and ADHD on your life.

Strategies for developing self-care practices that work for you

Strategies for developing self-care practices that work for you

Self-care is a crucial aspect of managing complex trauma and ADHD. With these conditions, it can be easy to neglect self-care practices, leading to increased stress, anxiety, and other symptoms. However, developing a self-care routine that works for you can significantly improve your overall well-being and quality of life. In this section, we will discuss strategies for developing self-care practices that work for you.

1. Start small – Developing a self-care routine can be overwhelming, especially if you are new to it. Start by identifying one or two self-care practices that you can easily incorporate into your daily routine. For example, you can start with taking a 10-minute walk every day or drinking a cup of herbal tea before bed.

2. Identify activities that bring you joy – Self-care should not feel like a chore. Identify activities that you enjoy and that help you relax. This can include reading a book, listening to music, taking a hot bath, or practicing yoga. Make time for these activities regularly.

3. Practice mindfulness – Mindfulness is a powerful tool for managing anxiety and stress. Incorporate mindfulness into your self-care routine by practicing deep breathing, meditation, or visualization exercises.

4. Prioritize sleep – Sleep is crucial for managing ADHD symptoms and improving overall well-being. Make sure you are getting enough sleep by establishing a consistent sleep schedule and creating a relaxing bedtime routine.

5. Connect with others – Social support is essential for managing complex trauma and ADHD. Make time to connect with friends and family, join a support group, or seek therapy.

6. Be kind to yourself – Self-care is about nurturing yourself. Be kind to yourself by practicing self-compassion and avoiding negative self-talk. Treat yourself with the same kindness and understanding that you would offer to a friend.

In conclusion, self-care practices are essential for managing complex trauma and ADHD. By starting small, identifying activities that bring you joy, practicing mindfulness, prioritizing sleep, connecting with others, and being kind to yourself, you can develop a self-care routine that works for you. Remember, self-care is not a one-size-fits-all approach, so experiment with different practices until you find what works best for you.

How self-care can improve symptoms of complex trauma and ADHD

How Self-Care Can Improve Symptoms of Complex Trauma and ADHD

Self-care is a term that has become increasingly popular in recent years, but what does it actually mean? Self-care refers to any activity that we do deliberately to take care of our physical, mental, and emotional health. It is not selfish or indulgent; it is essential for our well-being. For individuals dealing with complex trauma and undiagnosed ADHD, self-care practices can be particularly helpful in managing symptoms and improving overall quality of life.

Complex trauma and ADHD symptoms often overlap and can exacerbate each other. Symptoms such as hyperactivity, impulsivity, and difficulty concentrating can make it challenging for individuals to take care of themselves. However, by incorporating self-care practices into their daily routine, individuals can better manage their symptoms and improve their overall health.

One of the most effective self-care practices for individuals with complex trauma and ADHD is exercise. Exercise has been shown to improve mood, reduce anxiety, and boost cognitive function. Regular exercise can also help individuals with ADHD to better regulate their emotions and increase their ability to focus.

Another important self-care practice is getting adequate sleep. Sleep is essential for our physical and mental health, and lack of sleep can exacerbate symptoms of ADHD and complex trauma. Individuals should aim for at least seven to eight hours of sleep per night and establish a consistent sleep routine to help improve sleep quality.

In addition to exercise and sleep, mindfulness and relaxation techniques can also be helpful in managing symptoms of complex trauma and ADHD. Practices such as meditation, yoga, and deep breathing can help individuals to reduce stress and anxiety, improve focus and concentration, and increase overall feelings of well-being.

Self-care practices can also be helpful in managing executive dysfunction, a common symptom of both complex trauma and ADHD. Executive dysfunction refers to difficulties with planning, organization, and completing tasks. By incorporating self-care practices such as using a planner, breaking tasks into smaller steps, and setting realistic goals, individuals can better manage executive dysfunction and improve their ability to complete tasks and achieve their goals.

In conclusion, self-care practices are essential for individuals dealing with complex trauma and undiagnosed ADHD. By incorporating practices such as exercise, adequate sleep, mindfulness, and relaxation techniques, individuals can better manage their symptoms and improve their overall quality of life. It is important for individuals to prioritize their self-care and make it a part of their daily routine to improve their mental and physical health.

The Role of Medication in Managing ADHD Symptoms in Individuals with Complex Trauma

Overview of medication options

Overview of Medication Options

Medication is often a recommended treatment option for individuals with complex trauma and ADHD. It is important to note that medication should not be the sole treatment approach but should be used in conjunction with other interventions like therapy, lifestyle changes, and coping strategies.

Stimulant medications such as Ritalin, Adderall, and Concerta are often prescribed to manage ADHD symptoms. These medications work by increasing the levels of dopamine in the brain, which helps improve focus and concentration. However, stimulant medications can also have side effects like decreased appetite, difficulty sleeping, and increased heart rate.

Non-stimulant medications like Strattera and Intuniv are also used to treat ADHD symptoms. These medications work by increasing the levels of norepinephrine in the brain, which helps improve attention and impulse control. Non-stimulant medications have fewer side effects compared to stimulant medications, but they may take longer to start working.

It is important to work closely with a qualified healthcare professional to determine the most appropriate medication option for each individual. A healthcare professional will consider factors like age, medical history, and current symptoms before making a medication recommendation. It is also important to regularly monitor the effects of medication and adjust the dosage as needed.

Medication can be an effective tool in managing ADHD symptoms, but it is not a cure. It is important to combine medication with other interventions like therapy and lifestyle changes to achieve the best possible outcomes. Additionally, it is important to be aware of potential side effects and to communicate any concerns with the healthcare professional.

In conclusion, medication can be an effective treatment option for individuals with complex trauma and ADHD. It is important to work closely with a qualified healthcare professional to determine the most appropriate medication option and to regularly monitor the effects of medication. Medication should be used in conjunction with other interventions like therapy and lifestyle changes to achieve the best possible outcomes.

How medication can help with ADHD symptoms

Attention Deficit Hyperactivity Disorder (ADHD) is a neurodevelopmental disorder that affects millions of individuals worldwide. It is characterized by symptoms such as hyperactivity, impulsivity, and inattention. Individuals with complex trauma and undiagnosed ADHD may experience more severe symptoms, which can interfere with their daily functioning and quality of life. However, medication can help manage these symptoms and improve the individual's overall well-being.

Medication is a common treatment option for individuals with ADHD. It works by increasing the levels of neurotransmitters in the brain, which helps improve focus, attention, and impulse control. The most commonly prescribed medications for ADHD are stimulants such as Ritalin and Adderall. These medications are highly effective and can improve symptoms in up to 80% of individuals with ADHD.

For individuals with complex trauma and ADHD, medication can be particularly helpful. Studies have shown that individuals with a history of trauma may have a more severe form of ADHD, which can be more resistant to traditional treatments such as therapy and behavioral interventions. Medication can help manage these symptoms, making it easier for individuals to engage in other forms of treatment.

However, it is important to note that medication is not a cure for ADHD. It is only one part of a comprehensive treatment plan that should also include therapy, lifestyle changes, and other coping strategies. Additionally, medication can have side effects such as decreased appetite, insomnia, and irritability. These side effects can be managed by adjusting the dosage or switching to a different medication.

If you are considering medication for your ADHD symptoms, it is important to work with a qualified healthcare professional who can help you find the right medication and dosage for your individual needs. They can also monitor your progress and adjust your treatment plan as needed.

In conclusion, medication can be a valuable tool in managing ADHD symptoms in individuals with complex trauma. However, it should be used as part of a comprehensive treatment plan that includes therapy, lifestyle changes, and other coping strategies. If you are considering medication for your ADHD symptoms, it is important to work with a qualified healthcare professional to find the right treatment plan for you.

Finding the right medication and dosage

Finding the right medication and dosage is an important part of managing ADHD symptoms in patients with complex trauma. However, it can be a challenging process that requires patience, persistence, and collaboration with a healthcare professional.

The first step in finding the right medication is to undergo a thorough evaluation by a healthcare professional who specializes in treating ADHD. This evaluation involves a comprehensive medical history, a physical examination, and a series of tests to determine the severity of ADHD symptoms and the potential impact of complex trauma on these symptoms.

Once a diagnosis has been made, the healthcare professional will work with the patient to develop a treatment plan that may include medication, therapy, and lifestyle changes. Medication options for ADHD include stimulants and non-stimulants, and the right medication and dosage will vary depending on the individual's symptoms, medical history, and other factors.

It is important to note that medication is not a cure for ADHD, but rather a tool that can be used to manage symptoms. It may take several weeks or even months to find the right medication and dosage, and patience is key during this process. It is also important to communicate openly with the healthcare professional about any side effects or concerns that arise during treatment.

In addition to medication, therapy can also play an important role in managing complex trauma and ADHD. Therapy can help patients develop coping strategies, improve executive function skills, and address any underlying emotional or psychological issues that may be contributing to ADHD symptoms.

Self-care practices such as exercise, a healthy diet, and stress management techniques can also be effective in managing ADHD symptoms. Patients should work with their healthcare professional to develop a comprehensive treatment plan that includes medication, therapy, and lifestyle changes.

In conclusion, finding the right medication and dosage is an important part of managing ADHD symptoms in patients with complex trauma. It is a process that requires patience, persistence, and collaboration with a healthcare professional. By working together, patients can develop a treatment plan that addresses their unique needs and helps them manage their symptoms effectively.

The Impact of Childhood Trauma on ADHD Diagnosis and Treatment

Understanding how childhood trauma can impact ADHD diagnosis and treatment

Childhood trauma is a prevalent issue that affects many individuals, and it is known to cause significant effects on mental health and well-being. Attention Deficit Hyperactivity Disorder (ADHD) is a neurodevelopmental condition that affects individuals of all ages, and it is often diagnosed in childhood. However, childhood trauma can impact ADHD diagnosis and treatment, making it crucial for individuals to understand the link between the two.

Research has shown that childhood trauma can lead to changes in brain structure and function, affecting cognitive and emotional development. These changes can result in symptoms that overlap with ADHD, making it difficult to differentiate between the two conditions. For instance, individuals who have experienced childhood trauma may exhibit symptoms such as inattention, hyperactivity, and impulsivity, which are also typical of ADHD.

Moreover, childhood trauma can impact the severity of ADHD symptoms, making them more challenging to manage. Individuals who have experienced trauma may have difficulties with emotional regulation, which can exacerbate ADHD symptoms. Additionally, trauma can affect executive functions such as planning, organization, and decision-making, all of which are essential for managing ADHD symptoms effectively.

Therapy plays a crucial role in managing complex trauma and undiagnosed ADHD. Therapy can help individuals develop coping strategies for managing their symptoms, improve emotional regulation, and enhance self-awareness. Therapy can also help individuals develop healthy relationships and improve social interactions, which can be challenging for individuals with complex trauma and ADHD.

Self-care practices are also essential for individuals with complex trauma and ADHD. Self-care practices such as exercise, mindfulness, and healthy eating habits can help reduce stress and improve overall well-being. Furthermore, medication can be beneficial in managing ADHD symptoms in individuals with complex trauma. However, medication should be used in combination with therapy and other management strategies.

In conclusion, childhood trauma can impact ADHD diagnosis and treatment, making it crucial for individuals to understand the link between the two. Therapy, self-care practices, and medication can be effective in managing complex trauma and undiagnosed ADHD. It is essential for individuals to seek professional help and support to manage their symptoms effectively and improve their overall quality of life.

Strategies for managing childhood trauma and improving ADHD symptoms

Strategies for Managing Childhood Trauma and Improving ADHD Symptoms

Childhood trauma and ADHD can be a challenging combination to manage, but there are strategies that can help individuals cope and thrive. Here are some tips for managing executive dysfunction and improving ADHD symptoms in individuals with complex trauma and ADHD.

1. Seek therapy

Therapy can be a crucial component in managing childhood trauma and ADHD symptoms. A trained therapist can help individuals identify and work through the root causes of their trauma, develop coping mechanisms, and improve executive functioning skills.

2. Practice self-care

Self-care practices like exercise, meditation, and journaling can help individuals manage stress and regulate their emotions. It is important to make time for self-care activities that promote relaxation and self-reflection.

3. Develop a routine

Having a consistent routine can help individuals with ADHD manage their symptoms and stay on track with daily tasks. This can include establishing regular sleep patterns, scheduling time for exercise, and setting aside specific times for work and leisure activities.

4. Use organizational tools

Organizational tools like calendars, to-do lists, and reminders can be helpful for individuals with executive dysfunction. These tools can help individuals stay on top of tasks and manage their time more effectively.

5. Consider medication

Medication can be an effective tool for managing ADHD symptoms, but it is important to work closely with a healthcare provider to determine the right medication and dosage. Individuals with complex trauma may have unique considerations when it comes to medication, so it is important to discuss any concerns with a healthcare provider.

6. Build a support network

Strong social support can be invaluable in managing childhood trauma and ADHD. This can include family members, friends, or support groups. Having a support network can provide individuals with encouragement, accountability, and a safe space to discuss their experiences.

Managing childhood trauma and ADHD can be a challenging process, but with the right strategies and support, it is possible to improve executive functioning skills and thrive. By prioritizing therapy, self-care, routine, organizational tools, medication, and social support, individuals can develop a stronger sense of control over their symptoms and live fulfilling lives.

Conclusion

Recap of key points

Recap of Key Points

Throughout this book, we have discussed various strategies and techniques to help individuals with complex trauma and undiagnosed ADHD manage their symptoms and improve their overall quality of life. Here are some key points to remember:

1. The impact of complex trauma on ADHD symptoms and vice versa: Complex trauma can significantly affect ADHD symptoms, and vice versa. It is essential to understand the link between these two conditions to develop an effective treatment plan.

2. The role of therapy in managing complex trauma and undiagnosed ADHD: Therapy is crucial for individuals with complex trauma and undiagnosed ADHD. It can help them understand their emotions, develop coping skills, and improve their relationships.

3. Strategies for managing executive dysfunction in individuals with complex trauma and ADHD: Executive dysfunction is a common problem among individuals with complex trauma and ADHD. Developing strategies to manage these symptoms can help individuals improve their focus and productivity.

4. The link between complex trauma, ADHD, and anxiety: Individuals with complex trauma and ADHD often experience anxiety. Understanding the relationship between these conditions can help individuals develop effective coping strategies.

5. The impact of complex trauma and ADHD on relationships and social interactions: Complex trauma and ADHD can significantly affect an individual's relationships and social interactions. It is essential to work on communication skills and develop healthy relationships.

6. The importance of self-care practices for individuals with complex trauma and ADHD: Self-care is crucial for individuals with complex trauma and ADHD. Developing healthy habits can help individuals manage their symptoms and improve their overall well-being.

7. The role of medication in managing ADHD symptoms in individuals with complex trauma: Medication can be helpful for managing ADHD symptoms in individuals with complex trauma. However, it is essential to work with a healthcare professional to find the right medication and dosage.

8. The impact of childhood trauma on ADHD diagnosis and treatment: Childhood trauma can significantly affect ADHD diagnosis and treatment. It is essential to work with a healthcare professional who understands the complexities of these conditions.

In conclusion, managing complex trauma and undiagnosed ADHD can be challenging, but it is possible with the right strategies and support. It is essential to work with healthcare professionals and develop healthy habits to improve overall well-being. Remember that healing is a journey, and it takes time and effort, but it is worth it in the end.

Resources for further support

Resources for Further Support

Dealing with complex trauma and undiagnosed ADHD can be a challenging journey, but you do not have to go through it alone. There are several resources available to help you manage your symptoms and improve your quality of life. In this chapter, we will discuss some of the resources that you can access for further support.

Therapy

Therapy is an essential tool for managing complex trauma and ADHD. A therapist can help you identify your triggers, develop coping strategies, and improve your communication skills. There are different types of therapy available, including cognitive-behavioral therapy, dialectical behavior therapy, and eye movement desensitization and reprocessing (EMDR). You can work with your therapist to determine which type of therapy is best suited to your needs.

Support Groups

Support groups can provide a safe and supportive environment for individuals with complex trauma and ADHD. You can meet others who are going through similar experiences, share your thoughts and feelings, and learn from each other. Support groups can be found online or in person, and some are tailored specifically to individuals with ADHD or complex trauma.

Self-Care Practices

Self-care practices are essential for managing complex trauma and ADHD. These practices can help you reduce stress, improve your mood, and increase your overall well-being. Self-care practices include exercise, meditation, journaling, and spending time in nature. You can work with your therapist to develop a self-care plan that is tailored to your needs.

Medication

Medication can be an effective tool for managing ADHD symptoms in individuals with complex trauma. It is important to work with a qualified healthcare professional to determine if medication is right for you. Your doctor can help you find the right medication and dosage to manage your symptoms.

Childhood Trauma and ADHD

Childhood trauma can impact ADHD diagnosis and treatment. If you experienced trauma as a child, it is essential to discuss this with your doctor. Childhood trauma can impact brain development, which can lead to ADHD symptoms. Your doctor can work with you to develop a treatment plan that addresses both your ADHD symptoms and your trauma history.

Conclusion

Managing complex trauma and ADHD can be a challenging journey, but there are resources available to help you. Therapy, support groups, self-care practices, medication, and discussing your childhood trauma with your doctor are all important tools for managing your symptoms and improving your quality of life. Remember, you are not alone, and with the right support and tools, you can break through executive dysfunction and thrive.